Provinces and Territories of Canada

NORTHWEST TERRITORIES

— *"Spectacular"* —

Published by Weigl Educational Publishers Limited
6325 10 Street SE
Calgary, Alberta
T2H 2Z9

www.weigl.com

Library and Archives Canada Cataloguing in Publication data available upon request.
Fax 403-233-7769 for the attention of the Publishing Records department.

ISBN 978-1-55388-981-6 (hard cover)
ISBN 978-1-55388-994-6 (soft cover)

Printed in the United States of America
1 2 3 4 5 6 7 8 9 0 13 12 11 10 09

Editor: Heather C. Hudak
Design: Terry Paulhus

Every reasonable effort has been made to trace ownership and to obtain permission to reprint copyright material. The publishers would be pleased to have any errors or omissions brought to their attention so that they may be corrected in subsequent printings.

Weigl acknowledges Getty Images as one of its image suppliers for this title.
National Archives of Canada: page 30 top; Northwest Territories Archives: pages 29, 31 top; Terry Parker/NWTT: page 38.

All of the Internet URLs given in the book were valid at the time of publication. However, due to the dynamic nature of the Internet, some addresses may have changed, or sites may have ceased to exist since publication. While the author and publisher regret any inconvenience this may cause readers, no responsibility for any such changes can be accepted by either the author or the publisher.

We gratefully acknowledge the financial support of the Government of Canada through the Book Publishing Industry Development Program (BPIDP) for our publishing activities.

Contents

Northwest Territories

The Northwest Territories is sometimes described as Canada's last frontier. It is a place of wonder and beauty, with limitless space and open skies. Its untouched wilderness attracts many visitors who come to enjoy exciting outdoor activities such as hiking, fishing, bird-watching, and snowshoeing. The abundant and varied wildlife in the region also attracts visitors who wish to see interesting animals in their natural settings. There are more animals than there are people in the Northwest Territories. While the human population is small, a variety of cultures are represented throughout the region, including those of the Dene, Inuvialuit, and Métis. Many people living in the Northwest Territories have come from other parts of Canada looking for a simpler lifestyle.

The Northwest Territories covers 1,171,918 square kilometres—about 13 percent of the total area of Canada.

The border between the Northwest Territories and Nunavut runs through Melville Island and Victoria Island.

The Northwest Territories is one of Canada's three territories. The other territories are the Yukon, which lies to the west of the Northwest Territories, and Nunavut, which lies to the east. The provinces of British Columbia, Alberta, and Saskatchewan form the Northwest Territories' southern border, and the cold waters of the Arctic Ocean border it to the north. The Northwest Territories covers a huge amount of land, including a great deal of rugged, unpopulated wilderness.

Not only is the region home to Canada's longest river—the Mackenzie River—it is also home to two of the largest lakes in the world—Great Slave Lake and Great Bear Lake. The impressive Mackenzie mountain chain runs along the western border, and an endless variety of birds and wildlife live in the vast landscapes that make up the territory. Aboriginal Peoples were the first to live in the area that is now the Northwest Territories. Largely marine hunters, these peoples stayed close to the coastal regions.

In 1576, a British sea captain named Martin Frobisher arrived in the area. He started what was to become a long search for the Northwest Passage— a route for ships from the Atlantic Ocean to the Pacific Ocean that would allow easier trade with Asia. The search for the passage continued for more than 300 years.

The Mackenzie River is the tenth-longest river in the world.

Yellowknife became the capital of the Northwest Territories in 1967. It is the territory's only city and its largest community.

During the 1700s, two competing fur-trading companies, the North West Company and the Hudson's Bay Company, shared control over the Northwest Territories region. Both companies explored the area and established fur-trading posts. In 1821, the two ended their competition by merging under the name of the Hudson's Bay Company. Up until 1870, the region was part of British North America. In 1870, the Hudson's Bay's lands were renamed the North-West Territories and became part of Canada. These territories included what is now the Yukon, Nunavut, Alberta, Saskatchewan, and parts of Manitoba, Ontario, and Quebec.

The Yukon was part of the Northwest Territories until 1898.

The Northwest Passage has now been crossed a number of times, but it remains a difficult and challenging journey. Icebreaker ships are used to break through the ice that covers much of the passage.

On April 1, 1999, the Northwest Territories split into two distinct territories called the Northwest Territories and Nunavut.

The Northwest Territories is the second largest political unit in Canada. Nunavut, its eastern neighbour, is the largest.

The Northwest Territories is often referred to as being "north of sixty." This is because the north-south boundary that divides it from the provinces of British Columbia, Alberta, and Saskatchewan runs along the 60th parallel.

LAND AND CLIMATE

The Mackenzie River is a major Canadian waterway. For most of the year, this great river is cold, and its surface is frozen. However, during the short summer months, it is used as a transportation route.

The Northwest Territories has a varied landscape. The Interior Plains is mostly flat or gently rolling. This region is found between the territory's southern border and the Arctic Ocean. West of the Interior Plains is the Cordillera, which is a combination of mountains, valleys, and plateaus. East of the Interior Plains, the **Canadian Shield** dominates the landscape. Here, the rocks which form the rough, rugged terrain are some of the oldest in the world.

The territory's islands, including Prince Patrick and Victoria, are located in the Arctic Ocean and are part of the Arctic Lands region. These isolated masses of land are characterized by plains and plateaus.

The autumn season brings vibrant colours to some areas of the Northwest Territories.

Virginia Falls, located in Nahanni National Park, is twice the height of the famous Niagara Falls in Ontario.

The Northwest Territories is known for being cold all year round, and much of the ground is permafrost. Permafrost is permanently frozen ground. Only the thin top layer of the soil thaws during the summer.

The territory's climate is divided into two main zones—the Arctic and the subarctic. Both zones have very cold, long winters with temperatures often dropping as low as –50° Celsius. The Arctic zone's summers are short and cool, with average temperatures usually remaining below 10°C. The subarctic zone also has short summers, but temperatures often exceed 10°C. Sometimes, they can even reach 30°C.

GET THE FACTS

About 20 percent of the Northwest Territories is located within the Arctic Circle. Here, the sun shines for 24 hours on the summer solstice and never comes up on the winter solstice.

The highest named mountain in the territory is Mount Sir James MacBrien. It stands 2,762 metres high. There is a peak closeby that stands 12 metres higher than this, but it has no name.

NATURAL RESOURCES

Some people enjoy panning for gold and other minerals.

As a result of its cold climate, the Northwest Territories has almost no agricultural land. Permafrost slows growth and makes cultivation very difficult. However, the Northwest Territories does produce a large quantity of natural resources such as diamonds, zinc, and gold. The territory is rich in minerals and metals because much of it lies within the Canadian Shield.

Canada's first diamond mine, Ekati, opened in 1998, just northeast of Yellowknife. It produces about $450 million worth of diamonds each year. Production at the Diavik mine began in January 2003. By May, the mine had produced its first one million carats.

Float planes bring supplies to diamond camps.

Aboriginal Peoples sometimes use traditional methods to hunt.

Oil and gas are found in the Interior Plains and Arctic Lands regions. The Beaufort Sea is home to many large oil and gas reserves. Pipelines transport oil and gas from the Northwest Territories to British Columbia and Alberta.

In the Northwest Territories, fur is an abundant natural resource. Animals are hunted and trapped for their thick coats, which have developed in response to the cold environment. Lynx, fox, beaver, and polar bear are just a few of these animals. Fish are another important resource. Great Slave Lake is a popular spot for commercial fishing. There are few big fish, however, because the cold waters result in low reproduction rates and slow growth.

The territorial government regulates commercial fishing but does not interfere with the traditional fishing and hunting by the territory's Aboriginal Peoples.

Most of the gold deposits in the territory are around Yellowknife.

PLANTS AND ANIMALS

The jack pine is the official tree of the Northwest Territories.

The official territorial flower is the mountain avens, which is a member of the rose family.

The Arctic and the subarctic climatic zones of the Northwest Territories produce two very different plant regions. The two are divided by a tree line that can be traced from the Mackenzie River **delta** to the borders of Nunavut and Saskatchewan. North of the tree line, the arctic climate is too cold for most plant growth. Only strong, sturdy plants grow there, such as dwarf shrubs, grasses, moss, and heather. A sub-region of the Arctic Lands, known as the polar desert, is even more barren. Only lichens can survive the extremely bitter, dry cold. To the south, across the tree line and into the subarctic zone, the land becomes **taiga**. Summers in this region are warmer and more humid. The increased precipitation gives rise to lush plant growth, and trees survive to old age. Among these trees are black spruce, jack pine, birch, and aspen.

Lynxes live in the forests of the Northwest Territories.

The types of animals found in the Northwest Territories vary from region to region. Around the cold Arctic Lands, marine mammals feed on fish and other marine life. Walruses, narwhals, seals, beluga whales, and bowhead whales are often sighted in the deep blue ocean.

Caribou, arctic ground squirrels, arctic hares, muskox, and lemmings can all be found on the arctic **tundra**. Wolves are also common in this region because they follow the caribou herds north. Other **carnivores**, such as polar bears, arctic fox, and grizzly bears make their home north of the tree line as well. Polar bears stick close to the Arctic Ocean for their main source of food—seals.

White pelicans can be found along the Slave River. They are an endangered species.

KEEP CONNECTED

The gyrfalcon is the official territorial bird. To learn more about the gyrfalcon and other official symbols of the Northwest Territories, visit **www.pch.gc.ca/pgm/ceem-cced/symbl/101/119-eng.cfm**.

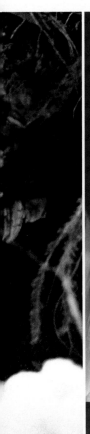

Whooping cranes are an endangered species that lives in Wood Buffalo National Park.

Muskoxen live in the Northwest Territories year long. Their fur is so thick that they are able to survive in temperatures as low as −40 ° Celsius.

North of the tree line, animals such as the arctic hare can often be spotted among the short, hardy plants that thrive in the region. Below the tree line, the subarctic zone is home to a wider variety of wildlife. More than 200 species of birds can be found there, along with black bears, deer, elk, moose, wolves, caribou, beavers, lynxes, muskrats, and red squirrels.

GET THE FACTS

Wood Buffalo National Park is the largest park in Canada and the second largest in the world, at 45,000 square kilometres.

If temperatures continue to rise in Arctic regions, many territorial animals will suffer. Bathurst caribou, muskox, Peary caribou, seals, sea lions, and walruses will all experience a decline in population. Polar bears will suffer the most, as longer ice-free periods will alter their feeding habits.

The Nahanni National Park Reserve is home to over 700 species of plants. This complex habitat exists because the park covers a variety of climatic zones.

The Northwest Territories is home to four national parks—Wood Buffalo and Nahanni lie in the south, and Tuktut Nogait and Aulavik are found in the north.

The snowy owl, the rock ptarmigan, and the raven are among the few birds that have adapted to the extreme temperatures of the territory and live there all year round.

The northern lights are a breathtaking sight, most clearly seen from dark locations "north of 60."

The Northwest Territories is most popular as a tourist destination during the summer months, when the weather is warmer. There is much to offer tourists in the summer. Hikers are attracted to the territory's four national parks, while fishers and hunters are drawn to its abundant wildlife. Many tourists come to bird-watch, while others prefer to watch for polar bears. Outdoor adventurers visit the area to take part in sports such as snowshoeing, cross-country skiing, snowmobiling, dog-sledding, ice-fishing, canoeing, white-water rafting, and horse trekking.

Some visitors enjoy learning about the traditional cultures of the Northwest Territories. Many festivals and museums provide tourists with the opportunity to find

The Wood Buffalo and Nahanni National Parks have both been named World Heritage Sites.

Visitors often travel to the Northwest Territories to experience its long summer days, midnight Sun, and explore the terrain.

out more about the history and culture of the Canadian North. Inuvialuit drum dancers perform their traditional songs and dances for crowds of travellers. The Caribou Carnival, another tourist-draw, is a three-day festival held in Yellowknife.

In Yellowknife, the end of winter is celebrated with the Caribou Carnival. Activities include dog-sled races, ice carving, ugly truck and dog contests, and snow canoe races.

INDUSTRY

Revenues from oil comprise 20 percent of total earnings for the territory.

The Northwest Territories' economy is very small. It contributes only one percent to Canada's total economy. There is no significant agricultural industry to be found in the Northwest Territories. The cold climate means that very little can be grown. Instead, the territory relies on its mineral industry for the majority of its economy. It exports lead, zinc, gold, diamonds, oil, and gas. Since the mid-1930s, Yellowknife has been a major producer of gold. This valuable metal, along with other non-renewable minerals abundant in the territory, is refined and processed for transportation to southern Canada and the United States.

KEEP CONNECTED

The territory is home to an abundant supply of diamonds, which have become a major contributor to the economy. To take a virtual tour of the Ekati mine from space, visit www.ccrs.nrcan.gc.ca/resource/tour/43/index_e.php.

The Northwest Territories' diamond mining industry is worth $2 billion.

Commercial fishing is a stable industry in the territory and is encouraged by the government. It is not a major contributor to the economy due to the high cost of transporting Arctic catches to southern markets.

GET THE FACTS

The Company of Cathay, led by Martin Frobisher in 1576, is famous for being Canada's first and most unsuccessful gold mining company. It was located on Kodlunan Island in Frobisher Bay.

The Giant Mine, a gold mine that closed in 1999, was instrumental in the economic growth of the Northwest Territories.

The Ekati diamond mine is responsible for creating 650 jobs since its opening in 1998.

The Con-Rycon mine in Yellowknife was the first major gold find in the Northwest Territories. Gold was discovered there in 1935, and the mine is still active today.

GOODS AND SERVICES

Snowmobiles are sometimes used to transport light cargo during the winter season.

Since the frozen ground makes agriculture almost impossible, airplanes are used to freight in the fruit and vegetables that are needed in the Northwest Territories.

Transportation plays an important role in the Northwest Territories. It provides job opportunities in the area, and allows the movement of goods to and from the territory. There is little manufacturing in the Northwest Territories so the oil, gas, gold, diamonds, and other materials are transported to other provinces. The transportation routes also function to bring in equipment, food, and materials that cannot be produced in the territory.

Manufactured products imported into the territory from elsewhere are generally shipped by air or by rail. Rail routes terminate at Hay River, where trucks often take over. Other cargo is transported via the Mackenzie River **barge** system. There are even winter ice roads between Fort Simpson and Fort Franklin on Great Bear Lake, and between Fort Norman and Norman Wells on the Mackenzie River.

The government employs 7,000 hospital workers, teachers, and civil servants.

Half of those employed in the service sector work for the federal, territorial, and local governments. Many others work in restaurants, hotels, and in retail. Dentists, doctors, accountants, and real estate agents find jobs in the more populated regions of the territory. Travel, tourism, and cultural education are the fastest growing industries in the territory. The government promotes growth in these areas in the hope of encouraging people to work and live in the region.

The Prince of Wales Northern Heritage Centre, in Yellowknife, is one of the best places to go for cultural education and information. It combines history, tradition, and culture with educational opportunities. There are databases, archives, and public records information available for anyone to use.

KEEP CONNECTED

To learn more about services offered in the Northwest Territories, as well as places to visit, check out **www.spectacularnwt.com**.

The cost of living in the Northwest Territories is at least 60 percent higher than in the rest of Canada.

The Mackenzie River has always been an important transportation route for the Northwest Territories. The river has determined the location of many communities.

The Prince of Wales Northern Heritage Centre has many programs that promote the territory's history. Travelling exhibits can be brought to any community in the territory for study and display.

Yearly events, such as the Diavik 150 Canadian Championship Dog Derby and Mining Week, allow the Northwest Territories' Aboriginal Peoples to celebrate their cultural roots.

In the 1950s, Byers Transport pioneered the concept of the ice road for the transportation of goods. During the darkest, coldest days of winter, they built a 520-kilometre road made entirely of ice and snow. It ran from Yellowknife to a silver mine above the Arctic Circle.

The Sunrise Festival takes place every January in Inuvik. It celebrates the first sunrise of the year.

The Northwest Territories offers many services for residents and tourists alike.

About 82 percent of the approximately 18,000 people employed in the Northwest Territories work in the service industry.

FIRST NATIONS

Present-day Inuit are descendants of the Thule.

Ancestors of the Dene lived in the area now called the Northwest Territories about 10,000 years ago, long before any European explorers arrived. Many separate groups made up the Northwest Territories' Dene peoples. Most of these had their own languages and lifestyles. The Yellowknife tribe of Dene were named for their use of yellow copper tools.

The Thule travelled in large whaling boats called umiaks. These boats were made from walrus ribs that had been covered in walrus hide. Umiaks could carry about 20 people at once.

Today, many of the Northwest Territories' Inuit and Dene continue to practise the traditional lifestyles of their ancestors.

Ancient Inuit ivory harpoon heads have been found in the Northwest Territories.

The Dene groups travelled and hunted under the leadership of the individual with the best hunting skills. The Dene were later joined by the Inuit. Inuit tended to live along the coastal areas of the territory because they relied heavily on whaling and hunting seals for their food and clothing. Archaeological evidence suggests that Inuit have lived in the territory for about 5,000 years.

The caribou has always been a very important animal to the Aboriginal Peoples of the Northwest Territories. It served as a source of food and clothing. It also appears in a great deal of Dene and Inuit religion and mythology.

EXPLORERS

While searching for the Northwest Passage, Henry Hudson and his crew became stuck in the ice. Some members of the crew became angry and set Hudson and several others adrift in a small boat, never to be seen again.

U p until the 1490s, most Europeans believed that the Arctic was covered in ice. An explorer named John Cabot questioned this belief by suggesting that there was a way through to Asia.

Beginning with Martin Frobisher in 1576, many European explorers came to the area in search of the **Northwest Passage**. William Baffin, who explored the Baffin Bay area, Alexander Mackenzie, whose namesake is the Mackenzie River, and Captain James Cook who navigated the western entrance, all hoped to cross the Arctic Ocean end to end.

The first person to cross the Northwest Passage was Norwegian explorer Roald Amundsen. He explored the North from 1903 to 1906.

Alexander Mackenzie explored the Northwest Territories by following the Mackenzie River to its mouth in the Arctic Ocean. His exploration paved the way for fur traders, who soon settled around the river.

Henry Hudson's first search for the Northwest Passage, in 1609, resulted in the discovery of the Hudson River. His expedition was considered the first to spend an entire winter in the Canadian North. Like this expedition, many other teams of explorers settled temporarily in the area as a result of their failure to find the Northwest Passage.

Sir John Franklin's Arctic expedition of 1845 resulted in significant Arctic exploration. Franklin's boats and crew disappeared among the icebergs and choppy freezing waters and were never seen again. Many expeditions were sent to find Franklin and his crew, resulting in much of the exploration and mapping of the region.

KEEP CONNECTED

Learn more about the history of the Northwest Territories at www.collectionscanada.gc.ca/confederation/023001-2245-e.html.

EARLY SETTLERS

In 1869, the Hudson's Bay Company lost its fur-trade monopoly when the territory was given to the new Dominion government in exchange for 300,000 British pounds.

The first permanent settlement on the Hay River was created in the 1890s, when Chief Chiatlo led a group there. They built log cabins and asked Anglican missionaries to join them. Today, this site is known as the Hay River Dene Reserve.

When the British government gave its territorial lands to the Hudson's Bay Company in 1670, it hoped that the fur trade would dominate the area. European explorers and fur traders were among the first to settle around the trading posts and waterways of the Arctic Ocean. Samuel Hearne, an employee of the Hudson's Bay Company, was the first European to arrive at Great Slave Lake. During the 1770s, his task was to find copper deposits. In the late 1770s, a rival trading company, the North West Company, sent Peter Pond to set up fur-trading posts along the Mackenzie River.

During the 1870s, the non-Aboriginal population in the Northwest Territories was around 7,000. It was made up almost entirely of hunters, trappers, or employees of the Hudson's Bay Company. As the economy relied on the fur trade, it was important that the population remained low.

The Hudson's Bay Company owned almost all of the Northwest Territories from 1670 to 1869. Employees of the company were among the territory's earliest European settlers.

The beginning of the 20th century was marked by rapid growth and change for the Northwest Territories. In 1873, the government of Canada created what is now the Royal Canadian Mounted Police (RCMP) to establish order across the country. In the Northwest Territories, they drove out troublesome hunters and trappers. Today, the RCMP remains the only police force in the territory.

The Northwest Territories continued to be overlooked even after the 1896 discovery of gold in Yellowknife. Prospectors who stopped in the area on their way to the Yukon found gold but considered the region too isolated. It was not until the 1930s and 1940s that the Northwest Territories opened up enough to provide access to these mineral discoveries. Once transportation routes were in place, settlers from elsewhere in Canada began to arrive. In the 1930s, radium

Shortly after World War II, large scale mines were erected in the Northwest Territories. Two major gold mines were built in the Yellowknife area, bringing many more settlers to the region.

was discovered in the Great Bear Lake region, and in 1934, the Yellowknife area was re-investigated for gold. By 1940, the population in Yellowknife had hit the 1,000 mark.

Between 1931 and 1941, the non-Aboriginal population of the Mackenzie region increased from 782 to more than 2,400.

In the planning stages, the RCMP were originally called the North West Mounted Rifles, but they had to change their name when the United States reacted to the idea of armed military patrolling their border.

Fort Norman was established in the 1920s after oil was discovered in the area.

Before the early 1960s, there were no roads linking Yellowknife to anywhere in the south.

When the Northwest Territories was owned by the Hudson's Bay Company, it was called Rupert's Land, after Prince Rupert, the son of King Charles II.

The 1850s saw Anglican and Catholic missionaries battling the cold weather and each other in a race to gain followers. Many churches were built around fur-trading posts and Aboriginal settlements.

POPULATION

Close to 19,000 people live in Yellowknife. Other communities in the territory include Inuvik, Hay River, Fort Smith, Rae, Fort Simpson, and Tuktoyaktuk.

There are more than 41,000 people living in the Northwest Territories. The population is unevenly spaced, with about two-thirds of the people living in the Great Slave Lake area. The Mackenzie Valley region contains almost one-third of the population, and the remaining areas are only sparsely populated.

The early European settlers in the Northwest Territories were mainly of British and French descent. German, Dutch, Greek, Italian, Lithuanian, Polish, and Scandinavian immigrants were also present in smaller numbers. Many of these early settlers stayed only temporarily. Today, only 25 percent of the population is of European descent.

While there are many Inuit living in the Northwest Territories, the majority live in Nunavut.

North of 60 degrees latitude, the caribou population outnumbers the human population.

The Northwest Territories has more than doubled in population since World War II. The construction of the Alaska Highway brought construction workers and made it easier to travel into the territory.

In 1953, the northern city of Aklavik was called "the town at the top of the world." During spring, when the ice broke up and melted, it would often flood. As a result, the Canadian government decided to move it 50 kilometres to the community of Inuvik.

There are eight official languages in the Northwest Territories. Many people speak English along with their traditional languages.

The Northwest Territories has a Language Commissioner who enforces official language laws.

Yellowknife's population is very culturally diverse. At least six different languages are spoken in the city.

POLITICS AND GOVERNMENT

The Legislative Building was built to reflect the culture of the Northwest Territories. The landscape around the building was preserved so that the animals living in the area could continue to thrive there.

The Legislative Assembly of the Northwest Territories is made up of 19 members who are elected by the people of the territory. Each member serves a four-year term. The assembly is headed by a commissioner and follows a system of consensus government. This means all members are free to vote independently on any issue. The approval of an issue relies on a majority vote. The executive council of the Legislative Assembly selects one of its members to be premier of the Northwest Territories.

The flag of the Northwest Territories is divided into three sections. There are two blue panels on either side of the centre, which is white and carries the territorial shield. The blue represents water, while the white symbolizes ice and snow.

The territory is represented by one elected member in the Canadian Parliament.

The territory's Legislative Assembly does not have the same powers as the Canadian provinces. The federal government controls most of the Northwest Territories' constitutional responsibility. However, the territorial government usually has the authority to make policies on territorial matters such as education, health care, housing, and social services.

Fort Smith sits on the 60th parallel and has a population of about 2,500. It was the territorial capital until 1967.

The territorial government is responsible for all health care and social services.

Before Nunavut became a separate territory in 1999, 24 members made up the Legislative Assembly of the Northwest Territories. After the split, that number went down to 14 members.

The Northwest Territories and Nunavut do not operate on the same party structure as the other provinces or the Yukon.

CULTURAL GROUPS

The Inuit build stone figures, which they call inukshuk. Traditionally, these large stone creations were used along trails to mark the way for fellow travellers and as a decoy to caribou.

Aboriginal Peoples make up about 50 percent of the population in the Northwest Territories. The three main groups are the Dene, the Inuit, and the Métis. The Dene are the largest Aboriginal group in the territory. They work to maintain their culture and share traditions with others. The Dene Cultural Institute, located in Hay River, relies on its strong oral tradition to preserve and teach its history and culture. Visitors to the institute can learn about the spiritual beliefs of the Dene, and observe Aboriginal arts, crafts, traditional storytelling, drumming, and dancing.

The Métis in the Northwest Territories are descendants of the Dene and European fur traders who first visited the region. Today, Métis in the territory maintain their cultural traditions with the help of several organizations. The Métis Nation is an organization that represents the interests of Métis people in the territory. Its head office is in Yellowknife. The North Slave Métis Alliance, also in Yellowknife, helps to promote Métis heritage and works to settle land claims.

Many Dene wear moccasins on their feet. Made from moose or caribou leather, these moccasins are decorated with colourful beadwork and traditional patterns, and trimmed with rabbit or beaver fur. They are warm and long-lasting.

The "dreamcatcher" is an Aboriginal art form that has become very popular around the world. Traditionally, this hand-crafted circle of grapevines was decorated with crystals and feathers. The webbing in the centre of the circle is believed to catch bad dreams, where they are held tight until the sunlight destroys them.

Soapstone carvings are an important art form for the Aboriginal cultures in the Northwest Territories. The carvings often represent animals or people from traditional stories and myths.

Another Aboriginal group in the Northwest Territories is the Inuvialuit, a subgroup of the Inuit. Most Inuvialuit speak Inuvialuktun and live along the territory's Arctic coast, or on Banks Island or Victoria Island. There are six other indigenous languages spoken in the Northwest Territories. These include Chipewyan, Dogrib, Gwich'in, Cree, North Slavey, and South Slavey. People in the Northwest Territories, both Aboriginal and non-Aboriginal, are proud of their territory and its heritage.

Many festivals and exhibits throughout the territory celebrate the various cultures and histories that are so much a part of the region. Yellowknife's Prince of Wales Northern Heritage Centre is the largest museum in the territory. It has a number of exhibits, including presentations on the early history of the area's Aboriginal Peoples, their languages, and traditions. Exhibits at the centre change regularly. Northern aviation, bush pilot history, and its role in establishing the territory has been featured in an exhibit. One of the earliest planes to fly in the North was among the displays in this exhibit.

ARTS AND ENTERTAINMENT

Folk on the Rocks is held every July along the shoreline of Long Lake, just outside Yellowknife. The festival attracts music enthusiasts from all over Canada and other parts of the world.

The Northwest Territories holds a number of entertaining events that draw large crowds. The Great Northern Arts Festival, held in Inuvik, brings together many Aboriginal cultures under one event. During this annual festival, more than 140 artists and entertainers from the Northwest Territories gather to offer a variety of perspectives through their art exhibitions and performances. There are paintings inspired by the northern lights, drawings inspired by the wilderness, photographs, carvings, hand-made jewellery, clothes, **tapestries**, and soapstone sculptures that reflect northern lifestyles.

Several smaller festivals are held across the territory. They often showcase many kinds of arts and crafts, including cooking, singing, drumming, dancing, sculpting, carving, traditional fiddling, and **throat-singing**.

The Snowking's Winter Festival is held each March in Yellowknife. The festival centres around a giant snow castle, built on Great Slave Lake.

Music thrives throughout the territory. Every year, Yellowknife hosts one of the biggest northern music festivals. Folk on the Rocks has been running since 1980 and features musicians from the Northwest Territories, the Yukon, Nunavut, and around the world. Each year, more than 65 performers appear on stage. Folk, blues, traditional, Celtic, rock, pop, and jazz music are all played using a variety of instruments.

While many northerners enjoy the art galleries, festivals, and concerts around the territory, entertainment is also found on the radio and television. CBC Television was first aired there in 1967. Since then, local news stations have been created to produce programs that reflect life in the Arctic. Some of these programs are produced in Aboriginal languages.

Many people visit the territory because it offers an excellent variety of recreational activities.

Visitors to Nahanni National Park can take white-water rafting tours that cover about 136 kilometres of rushing waters.

The Northwest Territories is an area of outstanding natural beauty. This makes it an ideal location for outdoor adventures. Whether suntanning on the beaches of its many lakes during the summer, or ice-fishing on the same lakes in the winter, activities in the territory are fun and exciting.

Nahanni National Park offers spectacular views of nature and wildlife. Outdoor enthusiasts can visit the park's natural hot springs or travel along the South Nahanni River by canoe, kayak, or raft. For those who enjoy a quicker pace, local outfitters offer white-water rafting tours. There are also many hiking trails in the park and in other areas of the territory. Other popular winter activities include snowshoeing, dog-sledding, skating, golfing, and ice-climbing. Other summer activities include hunting, cycling, and golfing.

Many visitors to the Northwest Territories are attracted by the first-class sport fishing.

The Arctic Winter Games are held every two years and bring northern nations together to participate and compete in various sports. Most activities are based on strength and agility, and showcase traditional skills. They include outdoor adventure sports such as ski biathlon, figure skating, skiing, hockey, and snowboarding. There are also events particular to Aboriginal traditions, such as snowshoeing, Dene games, Inuit games, and dog mushing.

Dog-sledding has been used as a form of transportation for hundreds of years, first by Aboriginal Peoples for travel and hunting, then by gold seekers to access difficult terrain and to transport goods. Today, many northerners participate in

KEEP CONNECTED

The logo for the Arctic Winter Games is made up of three interlocking rings, which represent social interaction, athletic competition, and cultural expression. To see the logo and learn more about the games, visit **www.arcticwintergames.org**.

Every year, Yellowknife holds the Super Soccer event. Many teams of boys and girls compete in indoor soccer for fun and prizes.

recreational dog-sledding. The first annual Sleigh Dog Race was held in Yellowknife in 1955. The first prize of $50 was given to Alfred Drygeese, from the Northwest Territories, who finished the 65-kilometre race in just under five hours and 27 minutes. The race was such a success that by the following year, the first prize went up to $500. Today, the race is known as the Diavik 150 Canadian Championship Dog Derby.

GET THE FACTS

The Canol Heritage Trail is considered to be one of Canada's greatest wilderness walks. It runs along the old pipeline between the Yukon border and Norman Wells. The hike takes up to four weeks, and there are no facilities along the way.

In the summer, the beach at Fred Henne Park, just outside Yellowknife, is a popular spot for a swim.

The Diavik 150 Canadian Championship Dog Derby takes place every March. The race covers more than 240 kilometres of challenging terrain. Dog-sledding is now a World Cup event.

A 30-kilogram lake trout from Great Bear Lake and a 14.5-kilogram Arctic char from Tree River are world-record-breaking catches from the area.

The first Arctic Winter Games were held in 1970 in Yellowknife. About 500 athletes, coaches, and officials participated in what was considered a huge success. Present-day games attract more than 1,600 athletes, coaches, cultural performers, staff, and officials.

CANADA

Canada is a vast nation, and each province and territory has its own unique features. This map shows important information about each of Canada's 10 provinces and three territories, including when they joined Confederation, their size, population, and capital city. For more information about Canada, visit **http://canada.gc.ca**.

Alberta
Entered Confederation: 1905
Capital: Edmonton
Area: 661,848 sq km
Population: 3,632,483

British Columbia
Entered Confederation: 1871
Capital: Victoria
Area: 944,735 sq km
Population: 4,419,974

Manitoba
Entered Confederation: 1870
Capital: Winnipeg
Area: 647,797 sq km
Population: 1,213,815

New Brunswick
Entered Confederation: 1867
Capital: Fredericton
Area: 72,908 sq km
Population: 748,319

Newfoundland and Labrador
Entered Confederation: 1949
Capital: St. John's
Area: 405,212 sq km
Population: 508,990

SYMBOLS OF THE NORTHWEST TERRITORIES

FLAG

COAT OF ARMS

Northwest Territories
Entered Confederation: 1870
Capital: Yellowknife
Area: 1,346,106 sq km
Population: 42,940

Nova Scotia
Entered Confederation: 1867
Capital: Halifax
Area: 55,284 sq km
Population: 939,531

Nunavut
Entered Confederation: 1999
Capital: Iqaluit
Area: 2,093,190 sq km
Population: 531,556

Ontario
Entered Confederation: 1867
Capital: Toronto
Area: 1,076,395 sq km
Population: 12,986,857

Prince Edward Island
Entered Confederation: 1873
Capital: Charlottetown
Area: 5,660 sq km
Population: 140,402

Quebec
Entered Confederation: 1867
Capital: Quebec City
Area: 1,542,056 sq km
Population: 7,782,561

Saskatchewan
Entered Confederation: 1905
Capital: Regina
Area: 651,036 sq km
Population: 1,023,810

Yukon
Entered Confederation: 1898
Capital: Whitehorse
Area: 482,443 sq km
Population: 33,442

0 200 400 Kilometers
0 200 400 Miles

Baffin Bay

Alert

mere
and

Baffin
Island

Davis Strait

Iqaluit
(Frobisher Bay)

Ivujivik

Labrador
Sea

dson
Bay

NEWFOUNDLAND

Schefferville

Happy Valley-
Goose Bay

Island of
Newfoundland

Chisasibi
(Fort George)

Gander
Saint John's

QUEBEC

Sept-Iles

Gulf of
St. Lawrence

St. Pierre and
Miquelon (FRANCE)

Moosonee

Chibougamau

PRINCE
EDWARD
ISLAND

Sydney

NEW
BRUNSWICK

Charlottetown

Quebec

Fredericton

Sherbrooke

Saint
John

Halifax

Sudbury

Montreal

NOVA
SCOTIA

Ottawa

Lake
Ontario

Lake
Huron

Toronto
Hamilton
London

Lake Erie

FLOWER
Mountain Avens

TREE
Jack Pine

BRAIN TEASERS

Test your knowledge of the Northwest Territories by trying to answer these mind-boggling brain teasers!

1 Multiple Choice

What is the territorial flower?
a) wild rose
b) mountain avens
c) pacific dogwood
d) fireweed

2 Multiple Choice

Who were the first people to live in the area that is now the Northwest Territories?
a) Americans
b) Europeans
c) Aboriginal Peoples
d) Canadians

3 Multiple Choice

What is the capital of the Northwest Territories?
a) Fort Simpson
b) Inuvik
c) Fort Smith
d) Yellowknife

4 True or False?

A "dreamcatcher" is a decorated, hand-crafted circle of grapevines believed to catch bad dreams.

5 True or False?

Getting to the Northwest Territories is very easy. There are numerous airports, roads, and ships that can be used to reach the territory.

6 True or False?

If temperatures continue to rise in the Arctic regions, many animals, including polar bears, will suffer as longer ice-free periods will alter their feeding habits.

7 Make a Guess

What industry does the Northwest Territories rely on for its economy?
a) oil
b) agriculture
c) mining
d) forestry

8 Multiple Choice

Aboriginal Peoples make up what percentage of the population?
a) 20
b) 99
c) 50
d) 10

1. B, The territorial flower is the mountain avens.   2. C, Aboriginal Peoples were the first people to live in the area now known as the Northwest Territories.   3. D, The capital of the Northwest Territories is Yellowknife.   4. True   5. False, It is difficult to get to the Northwest Territories as it has poor road development, and only one major airport.   6. True   7. C, The Northwest Territories relies on the mining industry for its economy.   8. C, Aboriginal Peoples make up 50 percent of the population.

MORE INFORMATION

GLOSSARY

barge: a large, flat-bottomed boat used to ship heavy freight along waterways

Canadian Shield: a region of ancient rock that encircles the Hudson Bay and covers part of mainland Canada

carnivores: animals that eat the meat of other animals

delta: mud, sand, and soil deposited at the mouth of a river

Northwest Passage: a water route from the Atlantic Ocean to the Pacific Ocean through the northern coastal waters of North America

taiga: northern forests consisting of trees that produce cones

tapestries: heavy cloth woven by hand with delicate patterns and colours

throat-singing: using the throat to produce a bass sound while at the same time creating melody with the mouth

tundra: vast, open, treeless plains found in arctic regions

BOOKS

Kissock, Heather. *Canadian Sites and Symbols: Northwest Territories*. Calgary: Weigl Educational Publishers Limited, 2004.

Parker, Janice. *Yellowknife: The Diamond Capital*. From the Canadian Cities series. Calgary: Weigl Educational Publishers Limited, 2002.

Marshall, Diana. *Canada's Land and People: Northwest Territories*. Calgary: Weigl Educational Publishers Limited, 2008.

Tomljanovic, Tatiana. *Linking Canadian Communities: Mining*. Calgary: Weigl Educational Publishers Limited, 2008.

WEBSITES

The Government of the Northwest Territories
www.gov.nt.ca

Legislative Assembly of the Northwest Territories
www.assembly.gov.nt.ca

The Northwest Territories
www.kidzone.ws/geography/nwt/index.htm

Some websites stay current longer than others. To find more information on the Northwest Territories, use your Internet search engine to look up such topics as "Yellowknife," "Dene," "Hay River," or any other topic you want to research.

INDEX

Arctic Ocean 6, 8, 14, 26, 27, 29

Arctic zone 9, 13

Beaufort Sea 11

Canadian Championship
Dog Derby 43

caribou 14, 15, 25, 33, 36, 37

Caribou Carnival 17

CBC Television 39

Dene 4, 24, 25, 29, 36, 37, 42, 47

Dene Cultural Institute 36

diamonds 10, 18, 19, 21

dog-sledding 16, 17, 41, 42, 43

Franklin, Sir John 27

Frobisher, Martin 6, 19, 26

fur trading 7, 28, 31

gold 10, 11, 18, 21, 30, 31

Great Bear Lake 6, 21, 31, 43

Great Northern Arts
Festival 38

Great Slave Lake 6, 11, 29, 32, 39

Hay River 17, 21, 29, 32, 36

Hearne, Samuel 29

Hudson's Bay Company 7, 28, 29, 30, 31

ice roads 21, 23

Inuit 24, 25, 32, 36, 37, 42

Inuvik 23, 32, 33, 38, 46

Mackenzie River 6, 7, 8, 13, 21, 23, 26, 27, 29

Métis 4, 36

mining 19, 23, 46

Nahanni National Park 9, 15, 16, 41

northern lights 16

North West Company 6, 7, 29

Northwest Passage 6, 7, 26, 27

Nunavut 6, 7, 13, 32, 35, 39, 45

oil 11, 18, 21, 31, 46

Pond, Peter 29

Prince of Wales Northern
Heritage Centre 22, 23, 37

Royal Canadian Mounted
Police 30, 31

subarctic zone 9, 13, 15

Wood Buffalo National
Park 15, 16

Yellowknife 7, 10, 11, 17, 18, 19, 22, 23, 30, 31, 32, 33, 36, 37, 38, 39, 43, 45, 46, 47